Scrap Quilting, Strip by Strip

Kim Brackett

Martingale®
Create with Confidence

Scrap Quilting, Strip by Strip

©2013 Kim Brackett

Projects in this book have previously appeared in *Scrap-Basket Sensations* and *Scrap-Basket Surprises* (Martingale, 2011 and 2009, respectively).

Martingale®
19021 120th Ave. NE, Ste. 102
Bothell, WA 98011-9511 USA
ShopMartingale.com

Printed in China

18 17 16 15 14 13   8 7 6 5 4 3 2 1

Library of Congress Cataloging-in-Publication Data is available upon request.

ISBN: 978-1-60468-299-1

Mission Statement

Dedicated to providing quality products and service to inspire creativity.

Credits

PRESIDENT AND CEO: **Tom Wierzbicki**

EDITOR IN CHIEF: **Mary V. Green**

DESIGN DIRECTOR: **Paula Schlosser**

MANAGING EDITOR: **Karen Costello Soltys**

ACQUISITIONS EDITOR: **Karen M. Burns**

TECHNICAL EDITORS: **Dawn Anderson and Laurie Baker**

COPY EDITOR: **Tiffany Mottet**

PRODUCTION MANAGER: **Regina Girard**

COVER AND INTERIOR DESIGNER: **Connor Chin**

PHOTOGRAPHER: **Brent Kane**

ILLUSTRATOR: **Laurel Strand**

Contents

There's something about a scrap quilt that just makes me happy. The more fabrics I'm able to use in a quilt, the more I love it when it's finished. It's a visual treat to spy certain fabrics that were left over from a favorite project, picked up at an amazing quilt show, or given to me by a special friend.

Whether you've been quilting for years or have just begun your quilting journey, you already know that scraps really do multiply when you're not looking! If you have a mountain of scraps, you'll find a variety of projects to put them to good use. If you haven't (yet) collected enough scraps to put together into a quilt, you can always combine your scraps with precut bundles of 2½" strips, or strips cut from your stash fabrics or fat quarters.

Several years ago, I began cutting my scraps into 2½"-wide strips and storing them neatly in clear shoebox-sized containers. The ease and convenience of using precut strips has been well worth the effort. It's so much fun to grab a few strips and begin cutting squares and rectangles. I really don't miss having to iron each piece of fabric as I pull it from my stash, then refold it before getting to the fun part. So go ahead and give it a try. With all those nice precut strips and these 12 different quilt designs, you'll be able to turn that mountain of scraps into a mountain of treasured scrap quilts in no time at all.

~ Kim Brackett

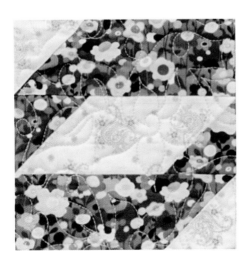

Each quilt "recipe" in this book contains a list of materials you will need to complete the quilt. The main ingredient in each list is an assortment of 2½"-wide strips. Following are some suggestions to help you build your collection of strips so that most of the cutting will be done before you begin your project.

- **Begin with your scrap basket.** If you're a serious quilter, you probably have lots of scraps left over from different projects, purchased in those irresistible grab bags, and given to you by family and friends. Dump your scraps onto a table or the floor and sort them into usable pieces (anything larger than 2½" square).

- **Sort through your stash fabrics.** If you have any fabrics that aren't destined to be a star in a quilt, consider cutting them into 2½"-wide strips to be used in scrap quilts. I have successfully combined calico fabrics from the 1980s with Civil War–era reproduction fabrics, and plaids with batiks!

- **Choose precut strips.** Some fabric manufacturers offer bundles or rolls of 2½"-wide strips that usually contain a strip from each fabric in a single collection. Using these collections will give your quilt a "designer" look. Precut bundles commonly contain 40 different fabric strips, and some of the quilts in this book require more strips than are in a precut bundle, but if you buy two of them, you can pick and choose your favorite strips for your project and use the leftover strips in another project later.

- **Join a strip club!** A "strip club" isn't what it sounds like! Your local quilt shop may offer a strip-of-the-month club. Customers pay a monthly fee for bundles of strips cut from new fabric bolts as they arrive in the shop. This is a great way to collect a variety of strips in styles and colors that you might not find in your stash.

- **Plan a strip swap.** Ask each guild or group member to bring a predetermined number of 2½"-wide strips to swap with others. Be sure that everyone is aware of any guidelines for the swap. You could also specify themes for certain months, such as Christmas strips for December, pink and red strips for February, and so on.

- **Shop for new fabrics.** After you have sorted your 2½"-wide strips and have chosen a project, select all the strips you think will work in that project. If you need more strips, or if you need a larger variety of fabrics for interest, take a trip to your local quilt shop or fabric store. Bring your strips with you, and then buy small amounts (a quarter of a yard) of fabrics that coordinate with the style and colors you already have. Cut these new fabrics into 2½"-wide strips. Use what you need for your project and store the others by style or color for use in future projects. If you're a new quilter, or if you just don't have any scraps, start from scratch and purchase whatever you like to make your quilt.

A bundle and rolls of precut 2½"-wide strips

Whether cutting from scraps or from yardage, follow the guidelines in this section to ensure that your strips and other elements of the quilt are cut accurately.

Cutting from Scraps

Iron your scraps to remove any wrinkles before cutting. Use spray starch for the more stubborn wrinkles and to add body and stability to the fabrics. Usually, you'll want to cut the longest strip possible. To even up the fabric for cutting, place the fabric scrap on your cutting mat so that the longest edge is vertical. Place your ruler on the fabric scrap near the right edge, following the grain line of the fabric and making sure that any uneven edges extend beyond the ruler. If it's difficult to determine where the grain line is, you may find it helpful to turn the scrap wrong side up, as the threads in the fabric seem more apparent from the wrong side. Cut along the right side of the ruler to trim off the uneven edges. Rotate your cutting mat 180° so that the straightened edge is now on your left. Place the 2½" mark of the ruler on the straightened edge of the fabric, and then cut along the right side of the ruler.

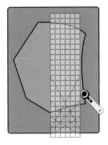 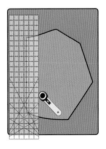

Continue making cuts in 2½" increments across the fabric. To save time, cut up to four or five scraps at once. Place the largest scraps on the bottom and until you run out of fabric.

Cutting from Yardage

Because the selvage edges shrink differently than the rest of the fabric, I like to remove these edges before cutting strips. Open the fabric and iron it to remove any wrinkles and to eliminate the original fold line. Fold the fabric in half with what were previously the selvage edges together, placing the folded edge nearest to you. Place a horizontal line toward the bottom edge of your ruler along the fold line. Cut along the right side of the ruler to even the edge of the fabric.

Rotate your cutting mat 180° so that the straightened edge of the fabric is on your left. (If you're cutting from fabric that is longer than your mat, gently fold the excess fabric onto the mat before rotating so that the fabric you just straightened doesn't move from its place on the mat.) Place the 2½" mark of the ruler on the trimmed edge and cut along the right side of the ruler to cut your strip. Continue to cut in 2½" increments until you have enough strips. **Note:** If you're left-handed, place the ruler on the left of the fabric for the straightening cut, and then rotate the mat so that you cut strips from the right edge of the fabric.

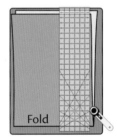 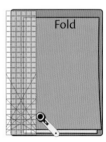

Crosscutting Strips

To cut a strip into smaller segments, trim the selvage edge so that it's straight and squared at a 90° angle. Using a small ruler, place the mark of the desired measurement on the left edge of the strip. Cut along the right side of the ruler. Continue to cut until you have the required number of pieces.

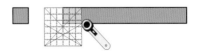

Triangle-free piecing techniques have been used throughout this book to create triangles and trapezoid shapes by using only squares and rectangles.

Folded-Corner Units

My two favorite methods for making folded-corner units are explained below; use whichever method works best for you.

Marking

Using a small ruler and a mechanical pencil, draw a diagonal line from corner to corner on the wrong side of a 2½" fabric square. Place the square on top of a fabric rectangle, right sides together and corners aligned, for folded-corner units (or on top of another square for half-square-triangle units) and sew on the drawn line. Fold up the square and match the corners and edges to make sure you've sewn accurately. If your corners don't meet, you may need to adjust your seam by sewing the width of a thread or two toward the upper corner. If your corners meet, press the triangle in place. Fold the triangle back down and trim the excess fabric, leaving ¼" seam allowances. Press back into place.

  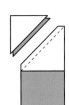

Sew on the diagonal line.   Check accuracy.   Trim seam allowances.   Press back into place.

No Marking

If you don't enjoy marking the diagonal lines on your folded corners, try making a temporary seam guide. Cut a piece of painter's tape about 3½" to 4" long. Place the tape on the bed of your sewing machine, lining up one long edge with the needle and making sure that the tape doesn't touch the feed dogs. Place the point of the unit to be sewn directly in front of the needle and make sure the other point is lined up with the edge of the painter's tape. Sew the unit, guiding the opposite point along the edge of the tape until it reaches the needle.

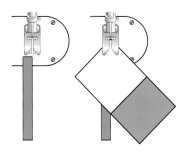

Split Units

Split units are similar to folded-corner units. Instead of sewing a square to a rectangle or another square, you sew two rectangles together at right angles to produce a unit that appears to be split diagonally in the middle. To make these units, place two fabric rectangles right sides together, at right angles, matching the corners. Draw a diagonal line from corner to corner. Sew on the drawn line. Fold the strip up and check to make sure you've sewn accurately. Trim the excess corner fabric, leaving ¼"-wide seam allowances. Press the seam allowances toward the darker fabric or press as indicated in the project instructions.

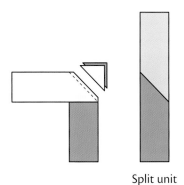

Split unit

Nova

Pieced by Kim Brackett; quilted by Karen Williamson

The blocks in this quilt appear to be offset, lending movement to the stars. To re-create this quilt, use a variety of batiks in subtle, muted shades.

Finished quilt: 61½" x 77½"   Finished block: 8" x 8"

Materials

Yardage is based on 42"-wide fabric.

32 strips, 2½" x 42", of assorted dark batiks for blocks

2⅓ yards of light batik for blocks

1⅓ yards of multicolored batik for outer border

1 yard of rust batik for inner border and binding

4¼ yards of fabric for backing

65½" x 81½" piece of batting

Cutting

From *each* of 16 assorted dark batik strips, cut:
  2 rectangles, 2½" x 8½" (32 total)
  1 rectangle, 2½" x 6½" (16 total)
  1 rectangle, 2½" x 4½" (16 total)
  4 squares, 2½" x 2½" (64 total)

From *each* of the remaining 16 dark batik strips, cut:
  1 rectangle, 2½" x 8½" (16 total)
  2 rectangles, 2½" x 6½" (32 total)
  2 rectangles, 2½" x 4½" (32 total)
  2 squares, 2½" x 2½" (32 total)

From the light batik, cut:
  30 strips, 2½" x 42"; crosscut into:
    48 rectangles, 2½" x 6½"
    336 squares, 2½" x 2½"

From the rust batik, cut:
  6 strips, 1½" x 42"
  8 strips, 2½" x 42"

From the multicolored batik, cut:
  7 strips, 6" x 42"

Cutting from Scraps

If you prefer to use scraps, follow the instructions below. See "Cutting" below left for instructions on cutting the borders and binding.

From assorted dark batiks, cut:
  48 rectangles, 2½" x 8½"
  48 rectangles, 2½" x 6½"
  48 rectangles, 2½" x 4½"
  96 squares, 2½" x 2½"

From assorted light batiks, cut:
  48 rectangles, 2½" x 6½"
  336 squares, 2½" x 2½"

Block Assembly

1 Referring to "Folded-Corner Units" on page 7 and using one dark batik and one light batik 2½" square, make a half-square-triangle unit. Press the seam allowances toward the dark triangle. Make 96.

Make 96.

2 Sew a light batik 2½" square to a dark side of a half-square-triangle unit from step 1. Press the seam allowances toward the square. Make 96.

Make 96.

3 Sew together two units from step 2. Press the seam allowances in a clockwise direction. Make 48.

Make 48.

4 Using a dark batik 2½" x 4½" rectangle and a light batik 2½" square, make a folded-corner unit as shown. Press the seam allowances toward the light triangle. Make 48.

Make 48.

5 Sew a unit from step 4 to a unit from step 3 as shown. Press the seam allowances toward the unit from step 4. Make 48.

Make 48.

6 Make a folded-corner unit as shown using a dark batik 2½" x 6½" rectangle and a light batik 2½" square. Press the seam allowances toward the light triangle. Make 48.

Make 48.

7 Sew a unit from step 6 to a unit from step 5 as shown. Press the seam allowances toward the unit from step 6. Make 48.

Make 48.

8 Sew a light batik 2½" x 6½" rectangle to the top of a unit from step 7. Press the seam allowances toward the rectangle. Make 48.

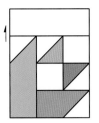

Make 48.

9 Make a folded-corner unit as shown using a dark batik 2½" x 8½" rectangle and a light batik 2½" square. Press the seam allowances toward the light triangle. Make 48.

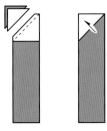

Make 48.

10 Sew a unit from step 9 to a unit from step 8 as shown. Press the seam allowances toward the unit from step 9. Make 48 blocks.

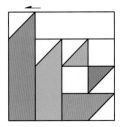

Make 48.

Quilt Assembly and Finishing

Go to ShopMartingale.com/HowtoQuilt for more information on any of the finishing steps.

1 Arrange the blocks in eight horizontal rows of six blocks each as shown. Sew the blocks together in rows, pressing the seam allowances in alternating directions from row to row. Sew the rows together. Press the seam allowances in the same direction.

2 Join the rust batik 1½"-wide inner-border strips and trim them to fit your quilt top. Sew the borders to the quilt top. Repeat for the multi-colored batik 6"-wide outer-border strips.

3 Layer the quilt top, batting, and backing; baste the layers together. Quilt as desired.

4 Use the rust batik 2½"-wide strips to bind the edges of the quilt.

5 Add a label.

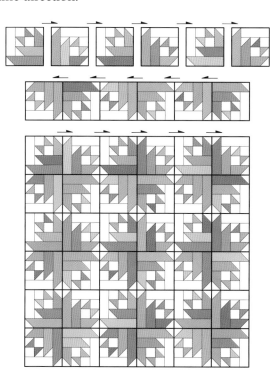

Mocha Swirl

Pieced and quilted by Karen Williamson

Karen used scraps in a rich palette of black, brown, and tan for this quilt. If you'd like to make a quilt from scraps like Karen's, follow the cutting instructions provided in the box "Cutting from Scraps."

Finished quilt: 57½" x 73½"   Finished block: 8" x 8"

Materials

Yardage is based on 42"-wide fabric.

1 yard of large-scale brown print for outer border

⅝ yard of black print for inner border

48 strips, 2½" x at least 34", of assorted black, brown, dark-tan, and light-tan prints for block backgrounds

24 strips, 2½" x at least 30", of assorted black, brown, dark-tan, and light-tan prints for stars

⅝ yard of brown print for binding

4 yards of fabric for backing

61½" x 77½" piece of batting

Cutting

From *each* of the 24 assorted strips for stars, cut:
   8 rectangles, 2½" x 3½" (192 total)*

From *each* of the 48 assorted strips for block backgrounds, cut:
   4 rectangles, 2½" x 4½" (192 total)
   4 rectangles, 2½" x 3½" (192 total)

From the black print for inner border, cut:
   8 strips, 2" x 42"

From the large-scale brown print for outer border, cut:
   8 strips, 3½" x 42"

From the brown print for binding, cut:
   7 strips, 2½" x 42"

You will have 2 sets of stars from each fabric strip.

Cutting from Scraps

If you prefer to use scraps, follow the instructions below. See "Cutting" below left for instructions on cutting the borders and binding.

Divide your scraps into two piles: those for stars and those for backgrounds.

From scraps for stars, cut:
   48 sets of 4 matching rectangles, 2½" x 3½" (192 total)

From scraps for backgrounds, cut:
   48 sets of 4 matching rectangles, 2½" x 3½" (192 total)
   48 sets of 4 matching rectangles, 2½" x 4½" (192 total)

Block Assembly

1 Choose a set of star fabrics (four matching 2½" x 3½" pieces) and a contrasting set of background fabrics (four each of matching 2½" x 3½" pieces and 2½" x 4½" pieces).

2 Referring to "Split Units" on page 7, construct a split unit using a star fabric 2½" x 3½" rectangle and a background fabric 2½" x 3½" rectangle. Press the seam allowances in either direction. Make four for each block.

Make 4
for each block.

3 Sew a split unit to a background 2½" x 4½" rectangle as shown. Press the seam allowances toward the background rectangle. Make four for each block.

Make 4
for each block.

4 Join the four matching units from step 3 as shown to complete one block. Press the seam allowances in a clockwise direction. Make 48 blocks.

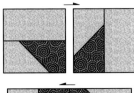

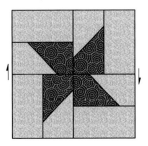

Make 48.

Quilt Assembly and Finishing

Go to ShopMartingale.com/HowtoQuilt for more information on any of the finishing steps.

1 Arrange the blocks in eight horizontal rows of six blocks each. Sew the blocks together in rows, pressing the seam allowances in alternating directions from row to row. Sew the rows together. Press the seam allowances in the same direction.

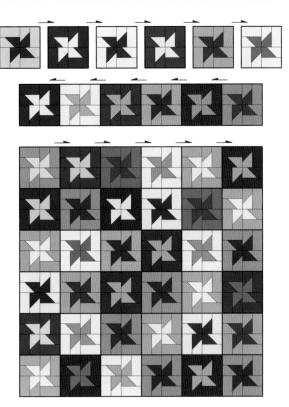

2 Join the black 2"-wide inner-border strips and trim them to fit your quilt top. Sew the borders to the quilt top, mitering the corners. Repeat for the large-scale brown 3½" outer-border strips.

3 Layer the quilt top, batting, and backing; baste the layers together. Quilt as desired.

4 Use the brown 2½"-wide strips to bind the edges of the quilt.

5 Add a label.

Beach Cottage

Pieced and quilted by Kim Brackett

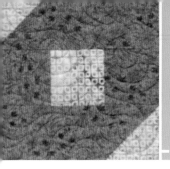

I selected low-contrast fabrics for this quilt because I wanted it to have a tranquil effect. If you want a bolder look, use fabrics with higher contrast.

Finished quilt: 60½" x 72½"   Finished block: 12" x 12"

Materials

Yardage is based on 42"-wide fabric.

2 yards of blue-and-green batik for outer border and binding

½ yard of blue batik for inner border

20 strips, 2½" x at least 28", of assorted medium-blue prints for blocks

20 strips, 2½" x at least 28", of assorted light-blue prints for blocks

20 strips, at least 2½" x 28", of assorted medium-green prints for blocks

20 strips, at least 2½" x 28", of assorted light-green prints for blocks

4¼ yards of fabric for backing

64½" x 76½" piece of batting

Cutting

From *each* of the 20 assorted light-blue print strips, cut:
  2 rectangles, 2½" x 6½" (40 total)
  5 squares, 2½" x 2½" (100 total)

From *each* of the 20 assorted medium-green print strips, cut:
  2 rectangles, 2½" x 6½" (40 total)
  5 squares, 2½" x 2½" (100 total)

From *each* of the 20 assorted medium-blue print strips, cut:
  2 rectangles, 2½" x 6½" (40 total)
  5 squares, 2½" x 2½" (100 total)

From *each* of the 20 assorted light-green print strips, cut:
  2 rectangles, 2½" x 6½" (40 total)
  5 squares, 2½" x 2½" (100 total)

From the blue batik, cut:
  8 strips, 1½" x 42"

From the blue-and-green batik, cut:
  8 strips, 5½" x 42"
  7 strips, 2½" x 42"

Cutting from Scraps

If you prefer to use scraps, follow the instructions below. See "Cutting" below left for instructions on cutting the borders and binding.

From light-blue scraps, cut:
  20 sets of:
    2 rectangles, 2½" x 6½" (40 total)
    2 squares, 2½" x 2½" (40 total)
  20 sets of 3 squares, 2½" x 2½" (60 total)

From medium-green scraps, cut:
  20 sets of:
    2 rectangles, 2½" x 6½" (40 total)
    2 squares, 2½" x 2½" (40 total)
  20 sets of 3 squares, 2½" x 2½" (60 total)

From medium-blue scraps, cut:
  20 sets of:
    2 rectangles, 2½" x 6½" (40 total)
    2 squares, 2½" x 2½" (40 total)
  20 sets of 3 squares, 2½" x 2½" (60 total)

From light-green scraps, cut:
  20 sets of:
    2 rectangles, 2½" x 6½" (40 total)
    2 squares, 2½" x 2½" (40 total)
  20 sets of 3 squares, 2½" x 2½" (60 total)

Block Assembly

Each quilt block is assembled from four smaller units. The smaller units are assembled in four different color schemes, labeled units A, B, C, and D. You'll need 20 of each.

1 For the A units, sew two light-blue 2½" squares to opposite sides of a medium-green background 2½" square. Press the seam allowances toward the light-blue squares.

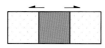

2 Sew light-blue 2½" x 6½" rectangles to the top and bottom of the unit from step 1. Press the seam allowances toward the light-blue rectangles.

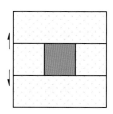

3 Place two medium-green 2½" background squares, wrong sides up as shown, on opposite corners of the unit from step 2. Sew a diagonal line, from corner to corner, across each square. Trim ¼" from the sewing lines. Press the seam allowances toward the medium-green triangles. Make 20 units using light blue as the main color and medium-green as the background color.

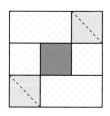 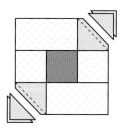

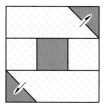

Make 20.

4 Repeat steps 1–3 to make B units in medium blue with a light-green background. Make 20.

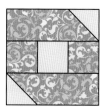

Make 20.

5 Repeat steps 1–3 to make C units in medium green with a light-blue background. Make 20.

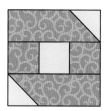

Make 20.

6 Repeat steps 1–3 to make D units in light green with a medium-blue background. Make 20.

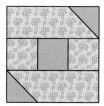

Make 20.

7 Join an A, B, C, and D unit as shown to construct one block. Press the seam allowances in a clockwise direction. Repeat to make 20 blocks.

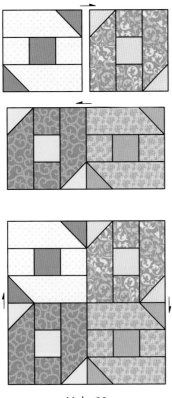

Make 20.

Quilt Assembly and Finishing

Go to ShopMartingale.com/HowtoQuilt for more information on any of the finishing steps.

1 Arrange the quilt blocks in five horizontal rows of four blocks each. Sew the blocks together in rows, pressing the seam allowances in alternating directions from row to row. Sew the rows together. Press the seam allowances in the same direction.

2 Join the blue 1½"-wide inner-border strips and trim them to fit your quilt top. Sew the borders to the quilt top. Repeat for the blue-and-green batik 5½"-wide outer-border strips.

3 Layer the quilt top, batting, and backing; baste the layers together. Quilt as desired.

4 Use the blue-and-green 2½"-wide strips to bind the edges of the quilt.

5 Add a label.

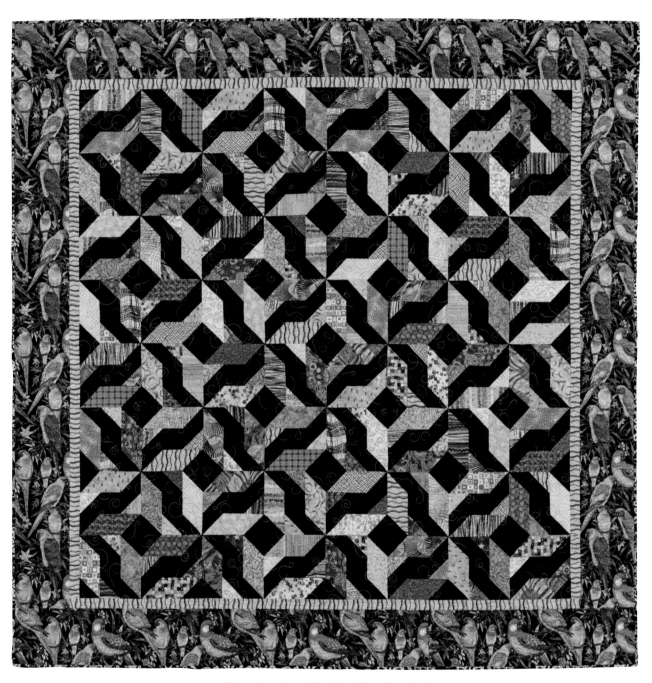

Pieced and quilted by Kim Brackett

I loved the bird print used in the border of this quilt, but I didn't notice that it was directional until I got it home. If you want to fussy cut a directional print, as I did, be sure to buy extra yardage.

Finished quilt: 61½" x 61½"   **Finished block: 12" x 12"**

Materials

Yardage is based on 42"-wide fabric.

2⅛ yards of black solid for block backgrounds

1½ yards of novelty print for outer border*

⅓ yard of striped green fabric for inner border

31 strips, 2½" x 42", of assorted bright prints for blocks

⅝ yard of black print for binding

4¼ yards of fabric for backing

65½" x 65½" piece of batting

*You'll need 2⅛ yards if your fabric is directional and you plan to fussy cut it as in the quilt shown.

Cutting

From the black solid, cut:
   28 strips, 2½" x 42"; crosscut into:
      64 rectangles, 2½" x 6½"
      256 squares, 2½" x 2½"

From the 31 assorted bright print strips, cut:
   128 rectangles, 2½" x 6½"
   128 squares, 2½" x 2½"

From the striped green fabric, cut:
   6 strips, 1½" x 42"

From the novelty print, cut:
   6 strips, 6" x 42"**

From the black print, cut:
   7 strips, 2½" x 42"

**If you have a directional print, cut 2 strips 6" x 48½" on the lengthwise grain, and then cut 3 strips 6" x 42" on the crosswise grain from the remaining fabric.

Cutting from Scraps

If you prefer to use scraps, follow the instructions below. See "Cutting" below left for instructions on cutting the borders and binding.

From bright print scraps, cut:
   128 rectangles, 2½" x 6½"
   128 squares, 2½" x 2½"

From scraps for backgrounds, cut:
   64 rectangles, 2½" x 6½"
   256 squares, 2½" x 2½"

Block Assembly

1 Referring to "Folded-Corner Units" on page 7, make a double folded-corner unit as shown using a black 2½" x 6½" rectangle and two bright print 2½" squares. Make 64.

Make 64.

2 Make a double folded-corner unit using a bright print 2½" x 6½" rectangle and two black 2½" squares. Make 128.

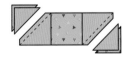 

Make 128.

3 Sew together one unit from step 1 and two units from step 2 as shown. Press the seam allowances toward the center. Make 64.

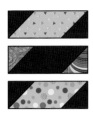

Make 64.

4 Join four units from step 3 as shown to construct one block. Press the seam allowances in a clockwise direction. Make 16 blocks.

Make 16.

Quilt Assembly and Finishing

Go to ShopMartingale.com/HowtoQuilt for more information on any of the finishing steps.

1 Arrange the blocks in four horizontal rows of four blocks each. Sew the blocks together in rows, pressing the seam allowances in alternating directions from row to row. Sew the rows together. Press the seam allowances in the same direction.

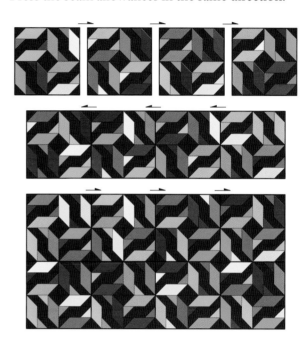

2 Join the striped green 1½"-wide inner-border strips and trim them to fit your quilt top. Sew the border strips to the quilt top. Repeat for the novelty print 6"-wide outer-border strips.

3 Layer the quilt top, batting, and backing; baste the layers together. Quilt as desired.

4 Use the black print 2½"-wide strips to bind the edges of the quilt.

5 Add a label.

Picnic

Pieced and quilted by Kim Brackett

Use contemporary prints for a quilt with a fun and fresh look, or choose another style or theme for a totally different effect. I'm itching to make this one with scraps of Christmas prints!

Finished quilt: 48½" x 60½"   Finished block: 6" x 6"

Materials

Yardage is based on 42"-wide fabric.

40 strips, 2½" x 42", of assorted dark prints for blocks

2 yards of light print for blocks

½ yard of multicolored print for binding

3½ yards of fabric for backing

52½" x 64½" piece of batting

Cutting

From each of the 40 assorted dark strips, cut:
4 rectangles, 2½" x 6½" (160 total)
4 squares, 2½" x 2½" (160 total)

From the light print, cut:
25 strips, 2½" x 42"; crosscut into:
80 rectangles, 2½" x 6½"
160 squares, 2½" x 2½"

From the multicolored print, cut:
6 strips, 2½" x 42"

Cutting from Scraps

If you prefer to use scraps, follow the instructions below, cutting the pieces in each set from the same fabric. See "Cutting" above for instructions on cutting the binding.

From assorted dark prints, cut:
80 sets of:
2 rectangles, 2½" x 6½" (160 total)
2 squares, 2½" x 2½" (160 total)

From assorted light prints, cut:
80 rectangles, 2½" x 6½"
160 squares, 2½" x 2½"

Block Assembly

1 Referring to "Folded-Corner Units" on page 7, make a double folded-corner unit as shown using a light 2½" x 6½" rectangle and two matching dark 2½" squares. Press the seam allowances toward the dark triangles. Make 80.

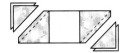 

Make 80.

2 Make a folded-corner unit as shown using a dark 2½" x 6½" rectangle and a light 2½" square. Press the seam allowances toward the light triangle. Make 160 in matching pairs.

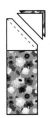 

Make 160.

3 Sew together one unit from step 1 and two matching units from step 2 as shown. Press the seam allowances toward the units from step 2. Make 80 blocks.

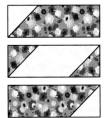 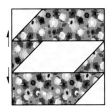

Make 80.

Quilt Assembly and Finishing

Go to ShopMartingale.com/HowtoQuilt for more information on any of the finishing steps.

1 Arrange the blocks into 10 horizontal rows of eight blocks each, rotating the blocks as shown. Sew the blocks together in rows, pressing the seam allowances as shown. Sew the rows together. Press the seam allowances in the same direction.

2 Layer the quilt top, batting, and backing; baste the layers together. Quilt as desired.

3 Use the multicolored print 2½"-wide strips to bind the edges of the quilt.

4 Add a label.

A Little Tangy

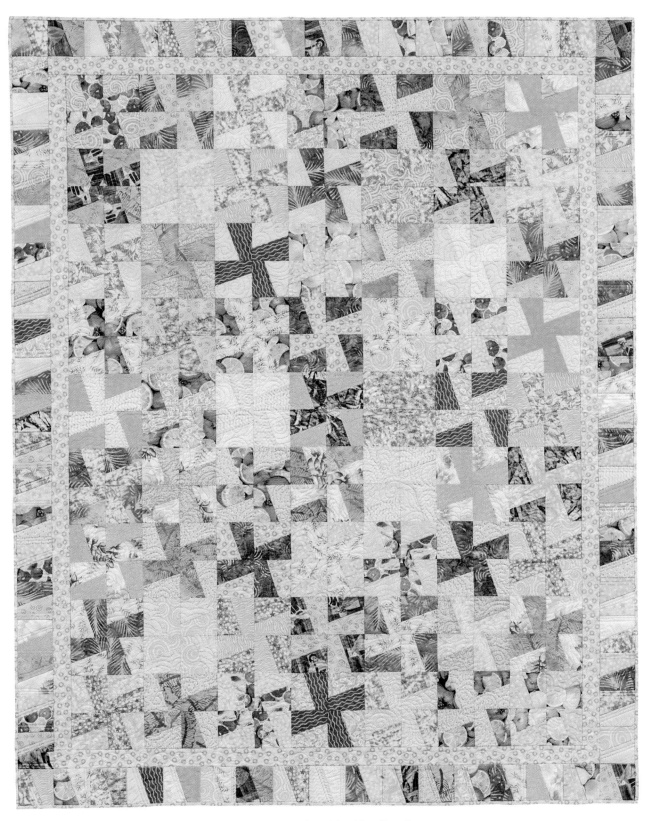

Pieced and quilted by Kim Brackett

This design was inspired by a lime-green scrap of fabric left over from a skirt that my mom made for my cousin. When I showed the quilt to my husband to elicit his comments, he declared it to be "a little tangy" for his taste.

Finished quilt: 51½" x 63½"   Finished block: 6" x 6"

Materials

Yardage is based on 42"-wide fabric.

1 yard of yellow print for inner border and binding

66 strips, 2½" x 42", of assorted yellow, orange, and green prints for blocks and outer border

3¾ yards of fabric for backing

55½" x 67½" piece of batting

Cutting

From the yellow print, cut:

6 strips, 2" x 42"

7 strips, 2½" x 42"

Cutting from Scraps

If you prefer to use scraps, cut two contrasting strips, 2½" x 18", for each block (4 units). See "Cutting" above for instructions on cutting the inner border and binding.

Block Assembly

The edges of every piece in this quilt will be cut on the bias. Be very careful when handling the quilt so that it doesn't stretch out of shape. You may find it helpful to use spray starch on your fabrics before cutting your 2½" strips. If you're using Jelly Rolls or other precut strips, spray them with starch *after* sewing the strips together in pairs. Once the blocks are cut, press only the seam allowances, avoiding touching the iron on the outside edges of the blocks. You may also want to stay-stitch (stitch ⅛" from the edges) around the perimeter of the quilt top to prevent stretching during the quilting process.

1 Sew two contrasting 2½" x 42" strips together lengthwise, extending the bottom strip by ½" as shown. Press the seam allowances in either direction. Make 33 strip sets.

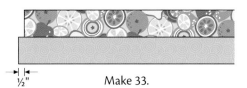

½"   Make 33.

2 Trace or photocopy the cutting pattern on page 27. Cut out the paper template around the outside edges. It should be 3½" square. Tape the template to the bottom of a 6½"-square ruler (or any ruler with a 3½" mark) with the right side of the template showing through the ruler. Place the ruler on the strip set so that the angled line in the middle of the template follows the seam line on the strip set. Cut along the right and top edges of the ruler. Rotate the cut piece to trim the remaining two edges as shown, placing the previously cut edges along the edge of the template. Cut 10 of these units from each strip set.

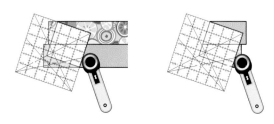

3 From 31 of the strip sets, use 8 of 10 matching units to construct pairs of blocks, with the fabric placement in one block the reverse of the other as shown. Construct a single block from one of the strip sets to make a total of 63 blocks. Press the seam allowances in a counterclockwise

direction. Set aside the leftover units for the outer border (six of the units will not be used).

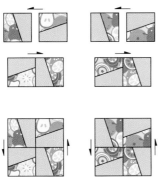

Make 63.

Quilt Assembly and Finishing

Go to ShopMartingale.com/HowtoQuilt for more information on any of the finishing steps.

1 Arrange the blocks in nine horizontal rows of seven blocks each. Sew the blocks together in rows, pressing the seam allowances in alternating directions from row to row. Sew the rows together. Press the seam allowances in the same direction.

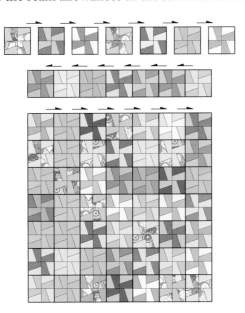

2 Piece together, end to end, the six yellow 2" x 42" strips. Cut two strips, 54½" long, and two strips, 45½" long. Join the 54½"-long strips to the sides of the quilt top. Press the seam allowances toward the inner border. Join the 45½"-long strips to the top and bottom edges of the quilt top. Press the seam allowances toward the inner border.

3 Join 19 leftover pieced units for each of the side borders and join 17 leftover pieced units

for each of the top and bottom borders. Press the seam allowances to one side. Join the side borders to the quilt top first, and then the top and bottom borders. Press the seam allowances toward the yellow inner border.

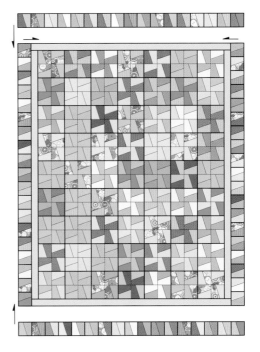

4 Layer the quilt top, batting, and backing; baste the layers together. Quilt as desired.

5 Use the yellow 2½"-wide strips to bind the edges of the quilt.

6 Add a label.

3½"

Cutting pattern

Place along seam line.

Snail Takes a Detour

Pieced and quilted by Kim Brackett

This Snail's Trail variation relies on contrast between the light and dark fabrics. Keep the contrast strong to enhance the design.

Finished quilt: 71½" x 71½"   Finished block: 8" x 8"

Materials

Yardage is based on 42"-wide fabric.

2 yards of novelty print for outer border and binding

⅜ yard of brown print for inner border

32 strips, 2½" x 42", of assorted dark prints in green, burgundy, and brown for blocks

32 strips, 2½" x 42", of assorted light-tan prints for blocks

5 yards of fabric for backing

75½" x 75½" piece of batting

Cutting

From *each* of 17 dark print and 17 light print strips, cut:

  2 rectangles, 2½" x 5½" (34 dark and 34 light total)

  5 rectangles, 2½" x 4½" (85 dark and 85 light total)*

  2 squares, 2½" x 2½" (34 dark and 34 light total)**

From *each* of 13 dark print and 13 light print strips, cut:

  2 rectangles, 2½" x 5½" (26 dark and 26 light total)

  4 rectangles, 2½" x 4½" (52 dark and 52 light total)*

  3 squares, 2½" x 2½" (39 dark and 39 light total)**

From *each* of 2 dark print and 2 light print strips, cut:

  4 rectangles, 2½" x 4½" (8 dark and 8 light total)*

  6 squares, 2½" x 2½" (12 dark and 12 light total)**

From the brown print, cut:

  7 strips, 1½" x 42"

From the novelty print, cut:

  7 strips, 6" x 42"

  8 strips, 2½" x 42"

You'll have a total of 145 dark and 145 light 2½" x 4½" rectangles; 1 rectangle of each won't be used.

**You'll have a total of 85 dark and 85 light 2½" squares; 1 dark square won't be used.*

Cutting from Scraps

If you prefer to use scraps, follow the instructions below. See "Cutting" at left for instructions on cutting the borders and binding.

From assorted dark prints, cut:

  60 rectangles, 2½" x 5½"

  144 rectangles, 2½" x 4½"

  84 squares, 2½" x 2½"

From assorted light prints, cut:

  60 rectangles, 2½" x 5½"

  144 rectangles, 2½" x 4½"

  85 squares, 2½" x 2½"

Block Assembly

1 Referring to "Folded-Corner Units" on page 7, make folded-corner units as shown, joining light 2½" x 4½" rectangles to dark 2½" squares and dark 2½" x 4½" rectangles to light 2½" squares. Make 72 of each, for a total of 144.

Light folded-corner unit. Make 72.   Dark folded-corner unit. Make 72.

2 Sew a dark 2½" x 4½" rectangle to each light folded-corner unit; sew a light 2½" x 4½" rectangle to each dark folded-corner unit as shown. Press the seam allowances toward the rectangles. Make 72 of each, for a total of 144.

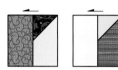

Make 72 of each.

3 Join two of each of the two units from step 2 as shown to complete one block. Press the seam allowances in a counterclockwise direction. Make 36 blocks.

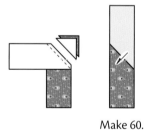

Make 36.

Sashing Unit Assembly

Referring to "Split Units" on page 7, make a split unit using a dark 2½" x 5½" rectangle and a light 2½" x 5½" rectangle. Press the seam allowances toward the dark fabric. Make 60 sashing units.

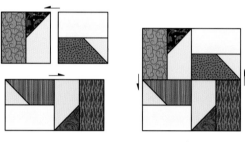

Make 60.

Quilt Assembly and Finishing

Go to ShopMartingale.com/HowtoQuilt for more information on any of the finishing steps.

1 Arrange the blocks, sashing units, and light and dark squares as shown. Sew the units together in rows, pressing the seam allowances as indicated by the arrows. Join the rows. Press the seam allowances in the same direction.

2 Join the brown 1½"-wide inner-border strips and trim them to fit your quilt top. Sew the borders to the quilt top. Repeat for the novelty print 6"-wide outer-border strips.

3 Layer the quilt top, batting, and backing; baste the layers together. Quilt as desired.

4 Use the novelty print 2½"-wide strips to bind the edges of the quilt.

5 Add a label.

Pieced and quilted by Kim Brackett

Using a solid white background allows even large-scale prints to stand out, and it provides a nice contrast for the main fabrics.

Finished quilt: 61½" x 61½"   Finished block: 12" x 12"

Materials

Yardage is based on 42"-wide fabric.

26 strips, 2½" x 42", of assorted dark prints in blues and greens for blocks

1⅛ yards of white solid for blocks

1⅛ yards of floral for outer border

⅓ yard of blue-and-green striped fabric for inner border

⅝ yard of blue-and-green print for binding

4¼ yards of fabric for backing

65½" x 65½" piece of batting

Cutting

From *each* of 20 assorted dark print strips, cut:
  4 rectangles, 2½" x 6½" (80 total; you'll have 2 left over)
  1 rectangle, 2½" x 4½" (20 total)
  2 squares, 2½" x 2½" (40 total)

From *each* of the remaining 6 assorted dark print strips, cut:
  3 rectangles, 2½" x 6½" (18 total)
  2 rectangles, 2½" x 4½" (12 total)
  4 squares, 2½" x 2½" (24 total)

From the white solid, cut:
  4 strips, 4½" x 42"; crosscut into 32 squares, 4½" x 4½"
  7 strips, 2½" x 42"; crosscut into 96 squares, 2½" x 2½"

From the blue-and-green striped fabric, cut:
  5 strips, 1½" x 42"

From the floral, cut:
  6 strips, 6" x 42"

From the blue-and-green print, cut:
  7 strips, 2½" x 42"

Cutting from Scraps

If you prefer to use scraps, follow the instructions below. See "Cutting" below left for instructions on cutting the borders and binding.

From assorted blue and green prints, cut:
  96 rectangles, 2½" x 6½"
  32 rectangles, 2½" x 4½"
  64 squares, 2½" x 2½"

From assorted light prints, cut:
  32 squares, 4½" x 4½"
  96 squares, 2½" x 2½"

Block Assembly

1 Referring to "Folded-Corner Units" on page 7 and using one blue or green print 2½" x 4½" rectangle and one white 2½" square, make a folded-corner unit as shown. Press the seam allowances toward the white triangle. Make 32.

Make 32.

2 Sew a folded-corner unit from step 1 to a white 4½" square. Press the seam allowances toward the square. Make 32.

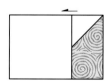

Make 32.

3 Make a folded-corner unit as shown using a blue or green print 2½" x 6½" rectangle and a white 2½" square. Press the seam allowances toward the white triangle. Make 32.

Make 32.

4 Sew a unit from step 3 to a unit from step 2. Press the seam allowances toward the unit from step 3. Make 32.

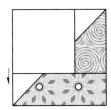

Make 32.

5 Sew blue or green print 2½" squares to the top and bottom of a white 2½" square. Press the seam allowances toward the blue or green squares. Make 32.

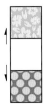

Make 32.

6 Sew blue or green print 2½" x 6½" rectangles to each side of a unit from step 5. Press the seam allowances toward the rectangles. Make 32.

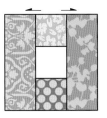

Make 32.

7 Sew together two units from step 4 and two units from step 6 as shown. Press the seam allowances in a clockwise direction. Make 16 blocks.

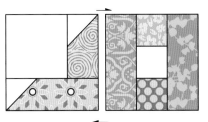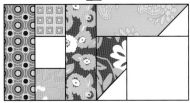

Make 16.

Quilt Assembly and Finishing

Go to ShopMartingale.com/HowtoQuilt for more information on any of the finishing steps.

1 Arrange the blocks into four horizontal rows of four blocks each as shown. Sew the blocks together in rows, pressing the seam allowances as shown. Sew the rows together. Press the seam allowances in the same direction.

2 Join the blue-and-green striped 1½"-wide inner-border strips and trim them to fit your quilt top. Sew the borders to the quilt top. Repeat for the floral 6"-wide outer-border strips.

3 Layer the quilt top, batting, and backing; baste the layers together. Quilt as desired.

4 Use the blue-and-green print 2½"-wide strips to bind the edges of the quilt.

5 Add a label.

Bali Sea Star

Pieced and quilted by Kim Brackett

If you're a little short on batik scraps, substitute a plain border for the pieced border. Just refer to the "Cutting from Scraps" box for the number of pieces to cut for the center stars and star outlines.

Finished quilt: 60½" x 72½"   Finished block: 12" x 12"

Materials

Yardage is based on 42"-wide fabric.

2½ yards of cream marbled print for blocks

1⅛ yards of brown marbled print for inner border and binding

51 strips, 2½" x 42", of assorted medium-dark to dark batiks for blocks and outer border

4¼ yards of fabric for backing

64½" x 76½" piece of batting

Cutting

From *each* of 20 of the assorted medium-dark to dark batik strips, cut:

4 rectangles, 2½" x 6½" (80 total)
2 rectangles, 2½" x 4½" (40 total)*

From *each* of the remaining 31 assorted medium-dark to dark batik strips, cut:

8 rectangles, 2½" x 4½" (248 total)*

From the cream marbled print, cut:

32 strips, 2½" x 42"; crosscut into:
80 rectangles, 2½" x 4½"
320 squares, 2½" x 2½"

From the brown marbled print, cut:

13 strips, 2½" x 42"

You'll have a total of 288 batik 2½" x 4½" rectangles; 4 rectangles will be left over.

Cutting from Scraps

If you prefer to use scraps, follow the instructions below. See "Cutting" below left for instructions on cutting the inner border and binding.

From assorted batiks, cut:

20 sets of:
4 matching rectangles, 2½" x 6½", for the center star of each block (80 total)
8 matching rectangles, 2½" x 4½", for the star outline of each block (160 total)
4 matching rectangles, 2½" x 4½" (80 total), and 16 matching squares, 2½" x 2½" (320 total), for the background of each block
124 rectangles, 2½" x 4½", for the outer border

Block Assembly

1 Referring to "Folded-Corner Units" on page 7, make a double folded-corner unit as shown using a batik 2½" x 4½" rectangle and two cream 2½" squares. Make four for each block.

Make 4
for each block.

2 Sew a batik 2½" x 4½" rectangle to a unit from step 1 as shown. Press the seam allowances toward the batik rectangle. Make four for each block.

Make 4
for each block.

3 Sew a cream 2½" x 4½" rectangle to a unit from step 2 as shown. Press the seam allowances toward the batik rectangle. Make four for each block.

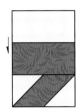

Make 4
for each block.

4 Make a double folded-corner unit as shown using a batik 2½" x 6½" rectangle and two cream 2½" squares. Make four for each block.

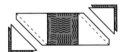 

Make 4
for each block.

5 Sew a unit from step 4 to a unit from step 3 as shown. Press the seam allowances toward the unit from step 4. Make four for each block.

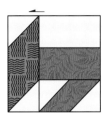

Make 4
for each block.

6 Join four of the units from step 5 as shown to complete one block. Press the seam allowances in a clockwise direction. Make 20 blocks.

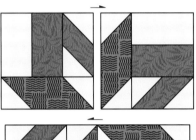

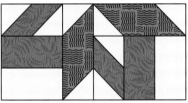

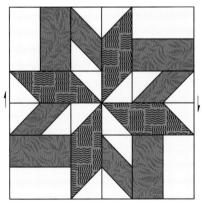

Make 20.

Quilt Assembly and Finishing

Go to ShopMartingale.com/HowtoQuilt for more information on any of the finishing steps.

1 Arrange the blocks in five horizontal rows of four blocks each. Sew the blocks together in rows, pressing the seam allowances in alternating directions from row to row. Sew the rows together. Press the seam allowances in the same direction.

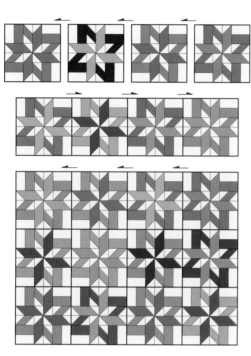

2 Piece together, end to end, six of the brown 2½" x 42" strips. Cut two strips, 60½" long, and two strips, 52½" long. Join the 60½"-long strips to the sides of the quilt top. Press the seam allowances toward the inner border. Join the 52½"-long strips to the top and bottom edges of the quilt top. Press the seam allowances toward the inner border.

3 Using the remaining batik 2½" x 4½" rectangles, piece the outer border as shown below. Add the side borders first, and then the top and bottom borders. Press the seam allowances toward the inner border.

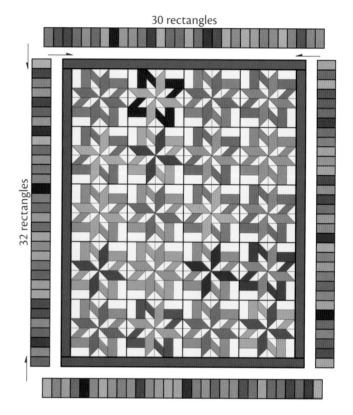

4 Layer the quilt top, batting, and backing; baste the layers together. Quilt as desired.

5 Use the remaining brown 2½"-wide strips to bind the edges of the quilt.

6 Add a label.

Pieced and quilted by Karen Williamson

The arrangement of this quilt center creates an illusion of layered blocks. If you aren't fond of pastel fabrics, use dark prints in place of the pastels, and a light background fabric in place of the dark brown.

Finished quilt: 64½" x 64½"   Finished block: 8" x 8"

Materials

Yardage is based on 42"-wide fabric.

64 strips, 2½" x at least 35", of assorted pastel prints for blocks

2⅜ yards of brown marbled print for blocks and binding

4½ yards of fabric for backing

68½" x 68½" piece of batting

Cutting

From *each* of the 64 pastel print strips, cut:
    1 rectangle, 2½" x 8½" (64 total)
    2 rectangles, 2½" x 6½" (128 total)
    2 rectangles, 2½" x 4½" (128 total)
    1 square, 2½" x 2½" (64 total)

From the brown marbled print, cut:
    31 strips, 2½" x 42"; crosscut 24 strips into 384 squares, 2½" x 2½". Set aside the remaining strips for the binding.

Cutting from Scraps

If you prefer to use scraps, follow the instructions below. See "Cutting" above for instructions on cutting the binding.

From assorted pastel prints, cut:
    64 rectangles, 2½" x 8½"
    128 rectangles, 2½" x 6½"
    128 rectangles, 2½" x 4½"
    64 squares, 2½" x 2½"

From assorted dark-brown prints, cut:
    384 squares, 2½" x 2½"

Block Assembly

1 Referring to "Folded-Corner Units" on page 7, make a half-square-triangle unit using a pastel 2½" square and a brown 2½" square. Press the seam allowances toward the brown triangle. Make 64.

Make 64.

2 Sew a brown 2½" square to a light side of a half-square-triangle unit from step 1. Press the seam allowances toward the brown square. Make 64.

Make 64.

3 Make a folded-corner unit using a pastel 2½" x 4½" rectangle and a brown 2½" square. Press the seam allowances toward the brown triangle. Make 128.

Make 128.

4 Sew together one unit from step 2 and two units from step 3 as shown. Press the seam allowances open. Make 64.

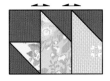

Make 64.

5 Make a double folded-corner unit as shown using a pastel 2½" x 6½" rectangle and two brown 2½" squares. Press the seam allowances toward the brown triangles. Make 64.

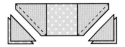

Make 64.

6 Sew a unit from step 5 to the bottom of a unit from step 4 as shown. Press the seam allowances open. Make 64.

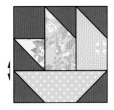

Make 64.

7 Sew a pastel 2½" x 6½" rectangle to the top of a unit from step 6. Press the seam allowances open. Make 64.

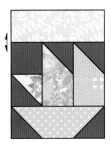

Make 64.

8 Sew a pastel 2½" x 8½" rectangle to one side of the unit from step 7 as shown. Press the seam allowances open. Make 64 blocks.

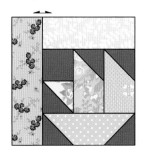

Make 64.

Quilt Assembly and Finishing

Go to ShopMartingale.com/HowtoQuilt for more information on any of the finishing steps.

1 Arrange the blocks into eight horizontal rows of eight blocks each, rotating the blocks as shown to form the design. Sew the blocks together in rows, pressing the seam allowances open. Sew the rows together. Press the seam allowances open.

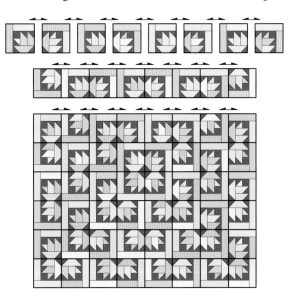

2 Layer the quilt top, batting, and backing; baste the layers together. Quilt as desired.

3 Use the seven remaining brown 2½" x 42" strips to bind the edges of the quilt.

4 Add a label.

Bali Breeze

Pieced and quilted by Kim Brackett

Use light and dark fabrics in any style or color for this easy-to-piece quilt. You'll be surprised by how quickly it goes together.

Finished quilt: 48½" x 60½"   Finished block: 6" x 6"

Materials

Yardage is based on 42"-wide fabric.

35 strips, 2½" x 42", of assorted light batiks for blocks

26 strips, 2½" x 42", of assorted dark batiks for blocks

½ yard of multicolored batik for binding

3½ yards of fabric for backing

52½" x 64½" piece of batting

Cutting

From *each* of 32 assorted light batik strips, cut:
 3 rectangles, 2½" x 6½" (96 total)
 4 rectangles, 2½" x 4½" (128 total)

From *each* of the remaining 3 assorted light batik strips, cut:
 6 rectangles, 2½" x 6½" (18 total; you'll have 2 left over)

From *each* of the 26 assorted dark batik strips, cut:
 5 rectangles, 2½" x 4½" (130 total; you'll have 2 left over)
 5 squares, 2½" x 2½" (130 total; you'll have 2 left over)

From the multicolored batik, cut:
 6 strips, 2½" x 42"

Cutting from Scraps

If you prefer to use scraps, follow the instructions below. See "Cutting" below left for instructions on cutting the binding.

From assorted light batiks, cut:
 112 rectangles, 2½" x 6½"
 128 rectangles, 2½" x 4½"

From assorted dark batiks, cut:
 128 rectangles, 2½" x 4½"
 128 squares, 2½" x 2½"

Block Assembly

1 Referring to "Split Units" on page 7, make a split unit as shown using a dark batik 2½" x 4½" rectangle and a light batik 2½" x 4½" rectangle. Press the seam allowances toward the light fabric. Make 128.

Make 128.

2 Referring to "Folded-Corner Units" on page 7, make a folded-corner unit as shown using a light batik 2½" x 6½" rectangle and a dark batik 2½" square. Press the seam allowances toward the dark triangle. Make 32.

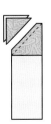

Make 32.

3 Make a double folded-corner unit as shown using a light batik 2½" x 6½" rectangle and two dark batik 2½" squares. Press the seam allowances toward the dark triangles. Make 48.

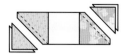 

Make 48.

4 To make block A, sew together a light batik 2½" x 6½" rectangle, a folded-corner unit from step 2, and a split unit from step 1 as shown. Press the seam allowances toward the light rectangle. Make 32 blocks.

 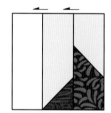

Block A.
Make 32.

5 To make block B, sew together two split units from step 1 and one double folded-corner unit from step 3 as shown. Press the seam allowances toward the double folded-corner unit. Make 48 blocks.

  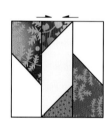

Block B.
Make 48.

Quilt Assembly and Finishing

Go to ShopMartingale.com/HowtoQuilt for more information on any of the finishing steps.

1 Arrange the blocks in 10 horizontal rows of eight blocks each as shown, placing the A blocks around the outside edges and the B blocks in the center. Sew the blocks together in rows, pressing the seam allowances as shown. Sew the rows together. Press the seam allowances in the same direction.

2 Layer the quilt top, batting, and backing; baste the layers together. Quilt as desired.

3 Use the multicolored batik 2½"-wide strips to bind the edges of the quilt.

4 Add a label.

Flowers for Nana Girl

Pieced and quilted by Karen Williamson

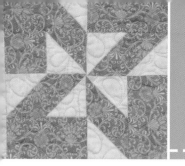

When Karen became a grandmother, she asked to be called "Nana," but soon after learning to talk, her granddaughter began calling Karen "Nana Girl."

Finished quilt: 56½" x 66½"   Finished block: 8" x 8"

Materials

Yardage is based on 42"-wide fabric.

20 strips, 2½" x 42", of assorted dark prints in pinks, reds, browns, and golds for blocks

2 yards of pale-yellow marbled print for blocks, sashing strips, and sashing posts

1⅓ yards of large-scale floral for outer border

½ yard of green print for sashing strip "leaves"

⅜ yard of brown print for inner border

⅝ yard of pink print for binding

4 yards of fabric for backing

60½" x 71½" piece of batting

Cutting

From *each* of the 20 assorted dark print strips, cut:

8 rectangles, 2½" x 4½" (160 total)

From the pale-yellow marbled print, cut:

13 strips, 2½" x 42"; crosscut into 49 rectangles, 2½" x 8½"

12 strips, 2½" x 42"; crosscut into 190 squares, 2½" x 2½"

From the green print, cut:

6 strips, 2½" x 42"; crosscut into 80 squares, 2½" x 2½"

From the brown print, cut:

5 strips, 2" x 42"

From the large-scale floral, cut:

7 strips, 6" x 42"

From the pink print, cut:

7 strips, 2½" x 42"

Cutting from Scraps

If you prefer to use scraps, follow the instructions below. See "Cutting" below left for instructions on cutting the borders and binding.

From assorted pink, red, brown, and gold prints, cut:

20 sets of 8 matching rectangles, 2½" x 4½" (160 total)

From assorted green prints, cut:

80 squares, 2½" x 2½"

From assorted light prints, cut:

49 rectangles, 2½" x 8½"

190 squares, 2½" x 2½"

Block Assembly

1 Referring to "Folded-Corner Units" on page 7 and using one dark 2½" x 4½" rectangle and two pale-yellow 2½" squares, make a double folded-corner unit as shown. Press the seam allowances toward the pale-yellow triangles. Make four identical units for each of the 20 blocks.

Make 4 for each block.

2 Sew a matching 2½" x 4½" rectangle to the top of each unit from step 1. Press the seam allowances toward the rectangles.

Make 4
for each block.

3 Sew together four matching units from step 2 as shown. Press the seam allowances as shown. Make 20 blocks.

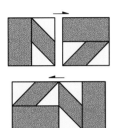
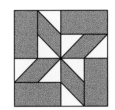

Make 20.

Sashing Strip Assembly

1 Using a pale-yellow 2½" x 8½" rectangle and a green print 2½" square, make a folded-corner unit as shown. Press the seam allowances toward the green triangle. Make 18.

Make 18.

2 Make a double folded-corner unit as shown using a pale-yellow 2½" x 8½" rectangle and two green print 2½" squares. Press the seam allowances toward the green triangles. Make 31.

Make 31.

Quilt Assembly and Finishing

Go to ShopMartingale.com/HowtoQuilt for more information on any of the finishing steps.

1 Arrange the blocks, pieced sashing strips, and pale-yellow 2½" sashing posts as shown. Sew the units together in horizontal rows, pressing the seam allowances as shown. Sew the rows together. Press the seam allowances in the same direction.

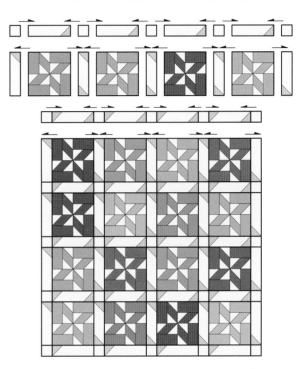

2 Join the brown 2"-wide inner-border strips and trim them to fit your quilt top. Sew the borders to the quilt top. Repeat with the floral 6"-wide outer-border strips, mitering the corners.

3 Layer the quilt top, batting, and backing; baste the layers together. Quilt as desired.

4 Use the pink print 2½"-wide strips to bind the edges of the quilt.

5 Add a label.

Kim Brackett lives in Gulf Breeze, Florida, with her husband and cats. She works full-time as a paralegal in Pensacola and is a member of the Pensacola Quilters Guild.

Kim developed an interest in quilting in 1988 after admiring a collection of vintage quilts displayed in an antique shop. She began gathering tools, fabrics, and patterns, and finally finished her first quilt 10 years later. Since then she has completed countless quilts, many of which have been featured in her books, *Scrap-Basket Surprises*, *Scrap-Basket Sensations*, and *Scrap-Basket Beauties* (Martingale, 2009, 2011, and 2013, respectively).